The Heart's Slow Race

The Heart's Slow Race

A Farewell To The Land

Poems and Photographs by
Galen Martini, O.S.B.

NORTH STAR PRESS

ST. CLOUD   MINNESOTA

Library of Congress Number: 76-024-956
International Standard Book Number: 0-87839-029-4

Some of the poems in this volume have appeared in *Carpenter, Beggar's Bowl, North Country Anvil, Northwoods Journal, Studio One.*
Copyright© 1976 Galen Martini, O.S.B. All rights in this book are reserved. No part of this book may be reproduced in any manner whatsoever without written permission except in the case of brief quotations embodied in critical articles or book reviews.

This book was typeset in 10/12 Caledonia by Media + Materials, Inc., St. Cloud, Minnesota; printed in the United States of America by The Sentinel Printing Company, St. Cloud, Minnesota; edition bound by the Midwest Editions, Inc., Minneapolis, Minnesota.

This first edition was published on July 31, 1976.

For further information address: The North Star Press, Post Office Box 451, St. Cloud, Minnesota 56301.

1 2 3 4 5 6 7 8 9 10

DEDICATION

This book is dedicated to S. Henrita Osendorf who loved me into finding my roots, to my uncle Tony who is in his person all that I know about love of the land, to my mother who gave me the gift of herself and her rich Slovenian ancestry, and to the memory of my father who while I was writing these poems burst upon heaven like a sky rocket July 4, 1973.

FOREWORD

This book grew out of four summers on the farm where my mother had grown up, and where her brother Tony still lives. The poems grew like seeds in the rich loam as I walked the land, trained a horse, communed with the trees and the shy old dog, and talked hours about the old times with my uncle. These summers, these experiences which became poems, knit together the poet and the peasant in me and I came from them a deeply whole woman.

My thanks to those at St. Benedict's, the women's Benedictine community to which I belong, who gave me the time and inner and outer space to let these poems be born in me.

Galen Martini, O. S. B.

CONTENT

My Uncle and I, We   1
Indian Soul   3
To Be One—Sun Prayer   5
Summer Memory   7
The Ground He Walked   9
The Heart's Slow Race   11
Echoes of You   13
Winter—Spring—Summer   15
Recognition   17
Snap Shot   19
Libation   21
Standing So   23
A Son Speaks   24
Clean—The Land   29
How Long the Land?   31
Spring Incantation   33
Song (For Meg)   35
Against the Setting of the Sun   37

My Uncle and I, We

My uncle and I, we
talk of the old
times. The ceaseless
chatter of bees in the old
orchard, the rasp
of an old saw mawing
at the marrow of the wood,
the bite of an old ax.

We talk, my mind's eye
remembering past the agony
of my birth, past the nine
months I lay hidden
devouring my mother's
strength, past the time
I lived between the genes
of my parents; remembering
with the memory born
of time impaled
inside me where my self
lives (curious as a bent
and ancient Indian—the keeper
of my self
hood, old
immovable ancient.)

My uncle and I, we talk—
one for an hour,
with the same curious,
implacable Indian (self
protector, medicine
man) living at our core.

Indian Soul

I am Indian
in my soul. Dark
red black sun
baked horseman lives
down there where I
live parched tight
in my white skin.
Anguished primitive lost
to the lush greenness
of the past stares out
of my eyes. When the sun
rises I bow reverent
as a dawning song. I am
Indian. When the keening
sun dies into the bleeding
lake I die
too, Indian to the soul,
dying as my race died
hounded into the dark
soil to be born again
        deep rain singing
        out of each cloud
        burst in summer.

To Be One—Sun Prayer

Like a whistling white
prayer it comes upon
me sudden—this longing
for the hard, fresh coldness
of snow, and snow packed
fields and bitter
winds and tears around
the eyes and breath
short, caught fast.
Like a prayer, like moths
beating against the light
I clamor inside
and grow quiet with sudden
longing to be one. To
be one with the wind
sound across the field
of white; and to be one
with the greenness
and the blazing blue skies.
Tight around the throat
draws the memory.
To be one, ah
to be one with the bay
gelding loping along
beneath me. Firm hoofed
over gravel and sand.
To be one.
       To be one.
To live one, unlined
by worry, healed strong
      by sun.

Summer Memory

My blue jeans hot
as a plaster cast, boots
clumping high
heels into dust, I walk
the path my mother used
to walk, a child in
the country. The buggy
tight in the old shed
is my stern grandfather's
now long dead whom
I missed all those years
before my birth. I miss
him yet—Slovenian
speech, strong in his
temper and his love.

My world is peopled
with dreamer men too
soft for live-coal eyes,
breaking the big studs, or
loving the feel of rough
log rooms. Strong,
lusty men, stern
for justice in their German
pride.

    I sit outside burning
in summer sun. Too
late for knowing the one
who fathered my hot
yearning and the poems
I write.

The Ground He Walked

Dodging the encounter (silence
lightninged with cocks' crows,
sparrows twittering, crickets
thrumming a background hum) dodging
the call of deep to deep, I stall, call
a friend (no answer) and at last
plunge into the farm
alone. Something in my breathing
whispers soon. My nerves like
crickets thrum that tune loud enough
for silence to hear. And suddenly
I am here walking the ground
my grandfather walked; siring
a family of two past a dozen. Every
cousin branching off from him
in endless variation. Like a theme
played numberless times upon
some different strings. I come
then, silence of this mystical
mystery night enclosing me green.
Black velvet green, golden green,
the scene speaks all in silence.
I stop talking to myself
long enough to shudder. The world
of centuries before me
too deep to utter.

The Heart's Slow Race

I suppose I wrote twenty
poems tonight caught
for a full half
hour in a hush
that brushes past
the telling. It was nearly
twilight, I walking
like a lone explorer,
or like some memory
of myself one
hundred ten years
ago as I roamed
this land in the body
of my ancestors. I love
them with a fierceness
born of the hush
tonight—the sun
glinting gold white
through some weeds
I found that in sun
gasp like diamonds.
(Ah, the sheen
of these wonder weeds,
the sheer glint
triggering the memory
back to birth and then
the sheer and precipitous
trip beyond.) Willows,
poplars, oaks, maples—one
gnarled dead trunk,
the top twisted beautiful
as an old man. I

stood, tears aching just
behind my throat, each
breath a kind of prayer.
(I used to think that
too dramatic, seeing it
on a page.) Seeing it in
my blood, heart's
slow race, I know
that I have never prayed
sheer, green and lithe
as I have this blinding,
binding day.

Echoes of You

You wore the rain lightly.
Like a cobweb stained
with light you
reached for me tenuous as
night. And then came morning

and a sky swimming in
sun. (I run
to music in my head. Only
melodies string the sound
soft enough between moments).

When you left the light
left too and it was night.
Tight as my ache was I saw
the marks of you around.
Darker than starlight. Stark
as a bear tree unleafed
in summer sun.

Now all the lonely land cries
out for you. I lie searching
a cloudless sky, watching
time run. Echoes come back
to me with setting of sun.

Winter—Spring—Summer

I stand remembering
as shadows color
the summer nearly
fall. Inside of me
solitude tears
like an ache
that is bittersweet
as the coming autumn.
Bitter as the dried
berries, sweet as new
tender corn. I remember

sun bleached days
I spent here, sick nearly,
with the color of the brilliant
light (memories of your harsh
eyes.) The hours
loping my long,
bay, (his soft
nose nuzzling as I brush
his silky coat.) The nights
tossing hour by hour past
midnight and beyond,
sleeping while roosters crowed
in the half light. Rambling
lonely as an owl
on the rooftops.

And the soft light
in your eyes when
reconciled we walked
the long path I'd spent
lonely hours trailing last
new mown winter-spring
summer.

Recognition

Grown old among the willows, broken
oaks and maples I find
myself. A sprightly girl
child grins at me from the top
of a gnarled oak. Choking back
the words, I do not call her down
from its branches. Chances
are this child grew there. Perched
there at two and grew from
sap and acorn into oak.

Older, pensive as a branch, pruned
by years of wear, there
walks the adolescent me. Stops,
examines, rambles on. No one
stops her. She stops no
one. Ever the mind tearing at the warp
of life. At last, sitting among
the daisies I find my present
self. Bent and gnarled, face
stained brown, older than an old
wet leaf. She looks at me ancient
eyes luminous, lit with wisdom
from within. I recognize each
nerve pulse. Sit, she beckons.

I reach for her among wooded paths
peopled, splintered with my past.

Snap Shot

And who recorded this
in God's mind, lens, camera;
shutter clinking with a slippery
click. Who caught it, etched
it on my mind, embossing
it green on green in the small
space that was me before birth.
It's there, though. I recognize
each leaf, each sun-locked
secret swims behind my eyes.
Clinking into place a second
before the shutter clicks.
My eyes float in wonder,
narrow before the sun. A Monarch
actually tries to sit on me; no
doubt it too remembers
me from the shadowless past.
We glide together on this patch
of earth my soul calls home.
I leave, packing my way back.
Power flows endlessly in me
as darkly deep,
as rich as garnered loam.

Libation

I have taken
to calling things by
their generic names. Here
puppy, I call, hey there
pony. It's all the same
to them. Flies examine
the jelly rolls I wolf
down loning it
on the prairie. A bee
threatens to eat me. Limb
upon limb leafs against
the sky. I leave one
bite of jelly as a prayer
against flies, bees, bad
weather, and move on.

Standing so

Hidden nearly, I
came upon the rusted
wheel and stood
quiet, still, wondering
what the wheel
had pulled. Snow drifts
was it put it rusted
here, or Spring thaw?

Ma, they called the wizened
lady wise with age, had
maybe said—it wriggles,
Anton, as it runs near sand.
Let it stand here, so, and find
a new to take-me to that
place. And so they chased
the hens away and set it
down. So. And took a new.

Still standing rusted to the tree,
I place my hand, so. Upon
                    my ancestry.

A Son Speaks

It started the way he
peeled me like a fruit
and laid me down
and whipped me there
in the old barn. Horses
raising frightened heads
at every whack of the harness
strap. I cried, yelled,
screamed and just
generally raised hell. The banty
hens squawked around like
crazies and wheeled
and fluttered. My mind

tried to think then when he
left me there blubbering
like a pot of boiling
soup. I had to stay an hour
in the dark barn to think,
he said. I shook my head
and waited for things to clear.
Big Dan, our draft horse, looked —
mild eyes examining
me as I examined my back
side. Black and blue
it would be. And did
I hate him for it? I stood
next to Dan and fondled
him and snuffed and wondered.
I'd stolen things
before but never this,
lying in my bed after lie
upon lie wove its way through
my stealing hands. I looked
at them in the darkness.
Big for a kid of ten.
But thin. Artist's hands my
father said. He'd laid me on
a bale of hay my mind
remembered. I heard the snapping
thwacks again. I stung

myself from thoughts of pain
and wondered did I hate
him. No, I thought. Who else
took chin in hand
and raised my head and looked
me clean in eyes that stuttered
and went dead. You did it,
Lad, he said. I nodded
numb; we walked together
silent to the barn. He'd talked
to me. Lad, he'd said,
(it was always Lad when
something bad had stolen
my name away). Lad, you're an
artist, with the fine mind
an artist needs to have. Don't
clutter it with lies. Stealing's
for the poor who haven't
riches stored and treasured
in their heads. I heard him
through a haze of tears his
gentleness had bred. The harness
only soothed my aching mind.
I loved him deep and rich

and smelling of hay I stood
my hour and shed bright tears
and bled my heart of every need
to steal. He came at ten.
Rustling in quiet as an old
worn dog. I turned. The lantern
etched scars of light into
my soul. Lad, he said.
I ran to him. He caught me up
in arms wide as our old bed stead.
I love you, Lad, my father said,
softer than chamois cloth, deeper
than my heart's blood red.

I cried my eyes sore
in his arms. Both of us
still and silent, warmth
running my spine like summer
showers. We walked together
to the house. My body light
as spun glass, my mind clean,
gold green; a hidden bower.

The Heart's Slow Race

Clean—The Land

Round as an onion,
peeled with tears, the years
have marked the stark
land with desire. Wire
fences, prickly thorns, hold
rapists out. Throughout
the farm, armed for safety
no alarm, no sound of barking
dogs keep clear the land.
Lovers of the soil stand
and nod and smile. While
near the allied house
the old pump stands and pumps
the clear, clean, living
        water out.

How Long the Land?

The evening lies like fog
upon the day. I stand
and walk and watch
and sing the kind of songs
that lone-men sing. I
dust my levis clean
of hay and watch the big
ones, bay and paint walk
with crisp hooves, heavy,
biting into clay. They
drink. Their large
eyes watch me for a
sudden sign that spells
unfriendly to their heavy
equine minds. I sit and chew
a stem of weed and whistle
through my teeth.

The evening lies like fog
upon the day. How long
will land lie free
and deep. Honest. Unyielding.
Yielding depths and sorrows,
riches cleaner than new rain.

Spring Incantation

He stood there solid
as old weathered oak,
busy taking root.
Overalls stained with
warmth and smell
of silage, jacket torn
below the elbow, brown
with age. Virgin forests
fell and rich loamed earth
began to grow. The family
started coming. Tony first,
small dreamer of farm dreams,
then Joe, then all of the dozen
others. Those were good
days he says. Bearded
and mustached, heavy with
strength, virile as the big
bay stud he stands there
taking root.

Roots. These are my roots,
I say, as I stand facing
the full barn, sit gazing
on family portraits, swing
my bay gelding into a soaring,
rollicking, rocking spring
canter.

Song
(For Meg)

I lie, warmth seeping
into heart pulsing, body
pounding; current of the earth.
I lie and sing my whole
being back to the land
from which I've sprung. Always
the leaf flowers into death
and back again to green. Life
throbs. I close my eyes, squint
one eye open and give myself
to the earth. A song starts
like a single flute note in my
heart and thunders through my bones.
Whole symphonies of wind trees
green boughs leaves swell
into sound. The wind dies

down. On a lone tree one
small bird sings its spirit
out against the sky.

Against the Setting of the Sun

Some night he'll feed the last
bay mare, worn wearily down with
pain he'll close tight the last
door, and slump uncomprehending
to the floor. It will come
that way. We know it he
and I. Unspoken, only in
our eyes we wear the pain.

Rain will come washing
this land down into the crater
of the past and gone. Long
shadows lie upon the final
hour. We see them hovering
like some lone eagle, claws
sharp, set to strike.

The end will come. It is
in sight. We shore our days
upon the land against
the landslide of the days to
come. We set our faces firmly,
yet weep against the setting
               of the sun.

PS   Martini, Galen.
3563
A7.335   The heart's slow race: a
H4   farewell to the land: poems
         and photographs

**NORMANDALE COMMUNITY
COLLEGE**
**9700 FRANCE AVENUE S.
BLOOMINGTON, MN 55431**